Little Monk's

Parvati

© Original text, Gauri Kelkar, 2011
Series Editor: Richa Jha

Illustrated by Shilo Shiv Suleman
Cover design by Shilo Shiv Suleman and Sandhya Sethumadhavan

ISBN: 978-81-8328-192-8

Published by
Wisdom Tree
4779/23, Ansari Road
Darya Ganj
New Delhi-110002
Ph.: 23247966/67/68
wisdomtreebooks@gmail.com

Printed in India at Print Perfect

TALES OF WISDOM
...UNIQUE VOCABULARY
ENHANCER...

Little Monk's

Parvati

Text
GAURI KELKAR

Illustrations
SHILO SHIV SULEMAN

wisdom
tree

Contents

Preface

· · · · · · ·

Parvati is considered to be the most prominent avatar of Goddess Durga. Parvati is the wife of Lord Shiva, the destroyer. She is the gentler and maternal version of the warrior-goddess, yet, skilled and powerful enough to destroy evil on Earth. In this avatar, she is a home-maker and a mother to gods Ganesha and Kartikeya, therefore easily identifiable with humans.

Parvati is the daughter of the lord of the mountains, Himavat, and a reincarnation of Lord Shiva's first wife, Sati, another avatar of Goddess Durga.

Parvati is variously referred to as Shailaputri, Ambika, Gauri, Shyama, Uma, Aparna among several others—Shyama, in her dark-skinned form, and Gauri, the golden-skinned one after having shed her skin following an intense penance.

She is depicted with two hands when she is with Lord Shiva, and with four when by herself.

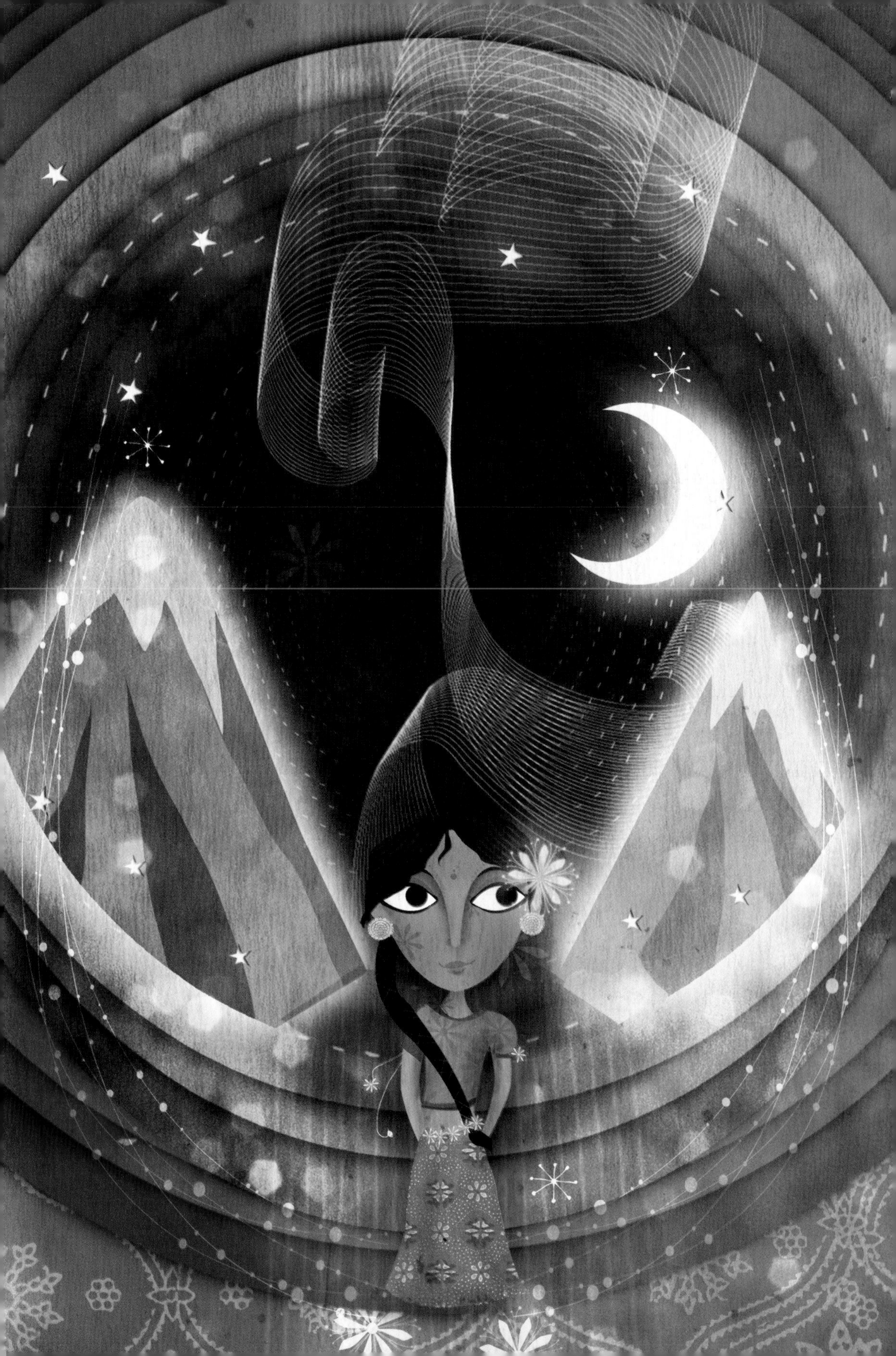

1
The Birth of Parvati

Once upon a time, Lord Shiva, who was part of the holy **trinity**, decided to **forego** his life as a **householder**. The great Lord had been utterly **devastated** by the death of his beloved wife, Sati. He lost interest in everything else. He went to a small **grove** in the Himalayas and began to live the life of a **hermit**.

A lot of time passed like this. Lord Shiva was deeply **absorbed** in meditation. He did not even notice the celebrations that were being organised one day near the grove where he was seated. Lord Himavat, the lord of the mountains and his wife, Menaka, had been blessed with a beautiful baby daughter. Everyone was **rejoicing** on this happy occasion. Lord Himavat could not contain his joy. He looked lovingly upon his daughter and told his wife Menaka, 'What a beautiful child! Our wish has been granted. We shall call her Parvati.' Everyone came to know her and love her as Parvati. But she was known by several other names as well. One of these was Shailaputri. And what was more, this was not her first birth! This beautiful girl had been Sati in her previous birth. The same Sati who was Lord Shiva's **consort** !

Sati herself was no ordinary girl. She was an **avatar** of Devi Durga herself. The Goddess had been pleased with King Daksha's **penances**. She had granted him the boon that she would be born to him. So it came to pass that Goddess Durga took birth as Sati. But King Daksha's arrogance **knew no bounds** when he **acquired** riches and became a powerful ruler. He had hurt and insulted Lord Shiva by not inviting him to a **ceremonial** sacrifice. Sati, **enraged** by this, had **vowed** to be reborn to a father she could be proud of, and had killed herself!

And so to fulfill Sati's **pledge**, the Goddess was born to Lord Himavat as Parvati.

However, Parvati's birth not only meant the **fulfillment** of Sati's wish—to be a daughter of a gentle, kind and affectionate father. It was also a sign of several things to come...

Parvati soon grew to be a beautiful young girl with **charming** manners. One day, the **divine** sage, Narad Muni visited Lord Himavat and saw Parvati. He **instantly recognised** that this young girl had in fact been born earlier as Sati! Narad Muni blessed her and told Himavat, 'O lord of the mountains, your daughter is **destined** to marry Lord Shiva.'

Himavat was thrilled to hear this. But he was also **puzzled**. After all, for several years Lord Shiva had been living a life of an **ascetic**. How was he ever going to notice his Parvati and fall in love with her?

Then Himavat had an idea. He spoke to Parvati, 'My dear child. I want you and your friends to serve Lord Shiva. He has spent many years meditating and I am sure he will **appreciate** some help so he can **concentrate** better.' Parvati readily agreed and went with her friends to **attend to** Lord Shiva. After gaining his permission, Parvati and her friends began to look after his needs.

Lord Shiva himself was only focusing on meditation and was **unaware** about the happenings around him. Even though he had allowed Parvati to serve him, he did not even notice her. Meanwhile, **unbeknownst** to both of them, frightening events were unfolding in Heaven *or devalok*!

The demons too had become aware of Lord Shiva's decision. They knew that without the great skills and ability of the Lord, the gods' army would lack strength. The time was **ripe** to launch an attack! So under the **charge** of the powerful demon king, Tarakasura, they began to spread terror in all the three worlds—Heaven, Earth and Netherworld or *patala*. Alas, they succeeded in defeating the gods and **drove them out** of Heaven.

Finally, to solve this latest **crisis**, the gods along with their king, Lord Indra, went to Lord Brahma for advice and **counsel**. 'O creator of the universe. Save us! The demon Tarakasura has become so powerful that he has now thrown us out of our kingdom. He treats our women like his maids and is **harassing** us. Give us a **commander** who can defeat this demon,' said Lord Indra anxiously.

Lord Brahma heard him out with some sympathy but he was helpless, 'O Indra. My hands are tied. It was my boon that has given Tarakasura so much power. But do not **fret**. There is but one way out of this.' Lord Indra and the other gods listened eagerly as Lord Brahma continued, 'Only a son born to Lord Shiva and Parvati, daughter of Lord Himavat, can destroy Tarakasura. It is certain that Parvati in this birth will be Lord Shiva's wife. Get him to notice her and all your problems will end.'

The gods were not sure of Lord Brahma's solution. After all, who would dare to break Lord Shiva's meditation and **risk** his anger! But with Lord Brahma's blessings, they **shook off** their doubts and began to think of a plan to marry Parvati and Lord Shiva.

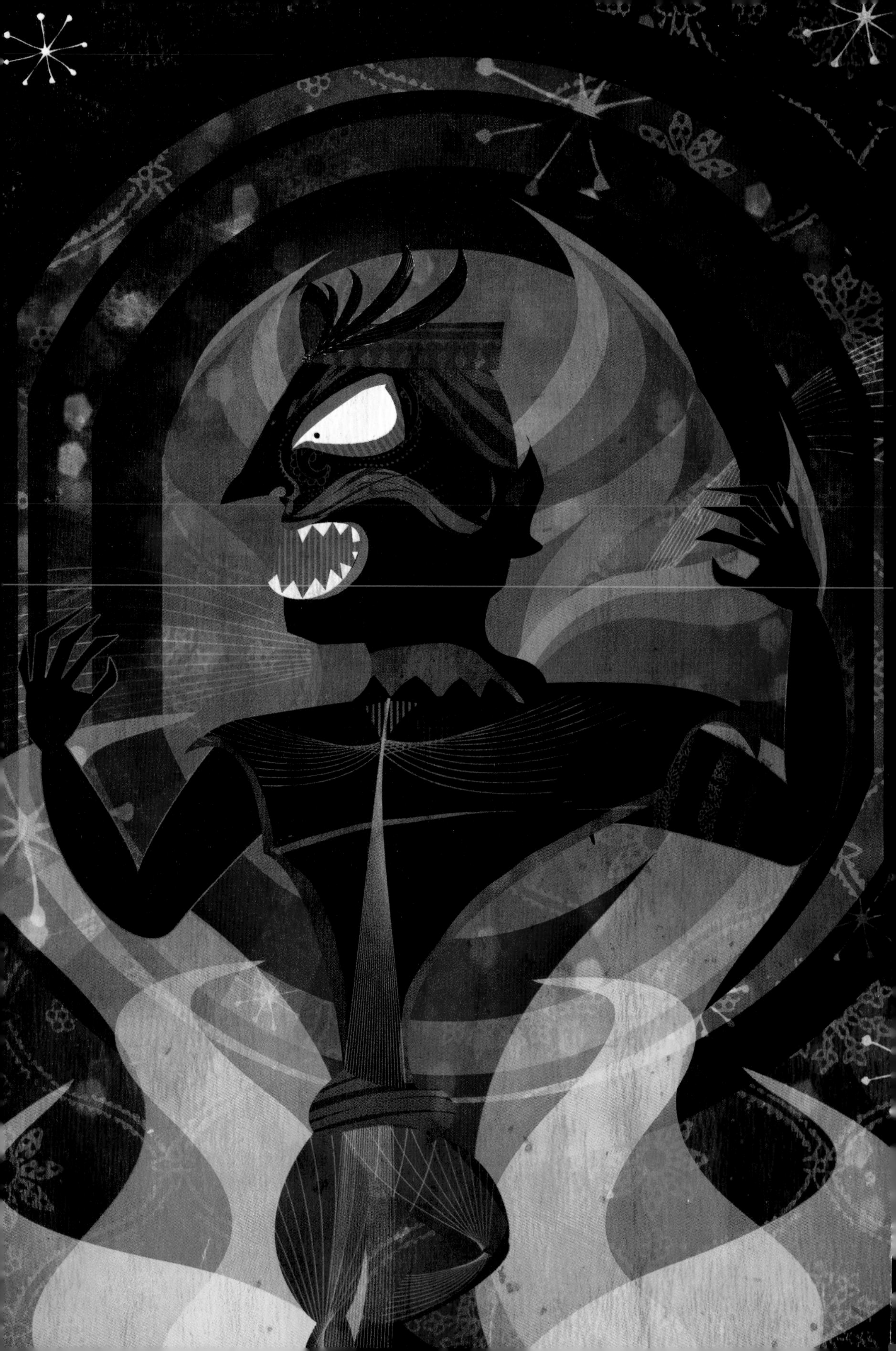

2
The Rise of Tarakasura
. . . .

While the gods were trying to find a solution to their **woes**, Tarakasura and his army were in a mood for celebrations. The demons were **euphoric** that they had an **edge over** the gods. It was a perfect opportunity to defeat their sworn enemies once and for all. And what was more, they had a strong leader as well—Tarakasura, who was feared by the gods themselves. As Tarakasura sat in his newly **conquered** kingdom, he thanked Lord Brahma for granting him the boons that gave him such strength!

Right from Lord Indra to Agnideva and the other gods, everybody was afraid of Tarakasura, who was the son of demon Vajranga and a beautiful **maiden** Varangi. A long time ago, Lord Brahma had created Varangi who later went on to marry Vajranga. One day, while she was meditating, Lord Indra **dared** to disturb her. This infuriated Vajranga and he went into a **severe** penance to take revenge against Lord Indra. Lord Brahma was pleased, and granted him his wish for a son who would defeat Lord Indra. This son was Tarakasura.

When Tarakasura was born, the very Earth began to **tremble**!

The oceans became stormy and the skies were filled with grey clouds. Even the smallest of living things **shuddered** at the thought of what was going to happen in the future. And the gods and mankind were nervous about the days ahead.

In due course, Tarakasura became the demon king and learned of Lord Indra's **misdeed**. He too decided to follow his father's footsteps. After **consulting** other demons, Tarakasura thought of **appealing** to his grandfather, Lord Brahma himself, for a boon that would help him defeat the gods. He went to meditate in the Madhuvana forest. As part of his penance, Tarakasura only drank water to satisfy his hunger. Then slowly, he filled his stomach with only air! He then stood in freezing cold water. Then he stood only on the thumb of his toe! He even stood on his hands with his legs up in the air. But Lord Brahma still did not appear. **Eventually**, flames began to **emerge** from Tarakasura's body! Finally, Lord Brahma had to **oblige**.

'O Tarakasura, tell me, what do you want?' Lord Brahma said. Tarakasura first requested that he should remain **immortal**. Lord Brahma rejected it saying that all living beings had to die. Then Tarakasura had a grand idea. He knew that Lord Shiva was **grieving** the death of his wife and was not interested in **worldly** matters any more. So he joined his hands and appealed, 'O Lord, grant me the boon that I shall only be killed by a son born to Lord Shiva. This boy should be a **mere infant** of seven days.'

Lord Brahma blessed him, 'So it shall be,' and disappeared. Tarakasura was confident that he could now escape death. Soon, with a mighty army of demons, he attacked the gods and drove them out of their kingdom. Little did he know that Lord Shiva's beloved Sati had been reborn as Parvati. Lord Shiva's period of **mourning** would soon draw to a close!

3
Kamadeva Turns to Ash

Tarakasura had indeed achieved his life-long ambition—to conquer Heaven. He thought he had finally defeated the gods for good, but they had not given up. While they started **plotting** ways to make Lord Shiva fall in love with Parvati, she herself had already fallen deeply in love with him.

Even though Lord Shiva spent all his time meditating and did not spare her a single **glance**, Parvati found herself drawn to him. She **gradually** lost interest in spending time with her friends…but alas! Lord Shiva did not seem to notice her at all.

It was around this time that the gods decided that the best way to make Lord Shiva fall in love with Parvati was to approach Kamadeva. After all, who would be better than the God of Love himself to help them in the matter!

So Lord Indra made his way to Kamadeva's **abode** and **narrated** the entire story, 'Lord we need your help. Lord Shiva is **oblivious** to Parvati who is serving as his maid. Please make him fall in love with her so that they can get married. Their firstborn is going to be our **saviour**.'

13

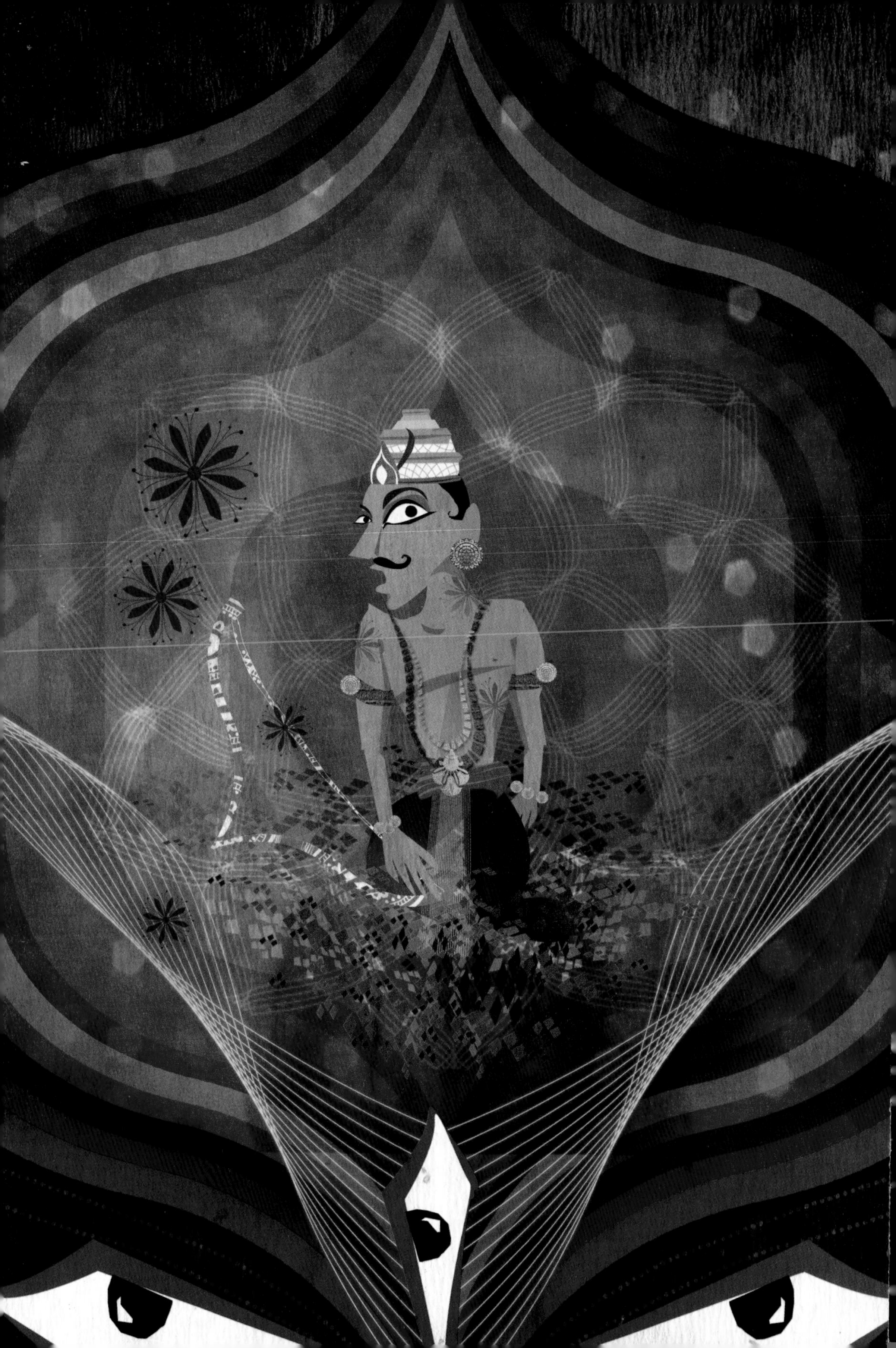

Kamadeva instantly agreed, and with his wife, Rati, made his way to the Himalayas. But as they got closer to where Lord Shiva sat, Kamadeva's courage seemed to fail him. He **confided** in Rati, 'I know I promised Lord Indra that I would help him, but…Lord Shiva has such an **unpredictable** temper! I do not think he will like being disturbed in such a manner. And besides, he is still mourning his beloved wife's death. How can I ….' But Kamadeva did not finish his thought.

At that instance, he saw Parvati. Her **radiant** beauty **reassured** him of the gods' plan. He told Rati, 'Dear wife, if that is Parvati, I do not think this task will be difficult!' 'Yes. I don't think you may have to do much at all!' Rati comforted her husband.

Kamadeva and Rati then quietly followed Parvati to the grove where Lord Shiva was sitting, but they stayed at a safe distance. Kamadeva watched very carefully as Parvati approached Lord Shiva, whose **grim** face again made him doubt himself. He **hesitated**. She put the flowers she had gathered at Lord Shiva's feet, and he opened his eyes. Kamadeva saw Lord Shiva looking at Parvati and thought to himself, 'It seems as though Lord Shiva, likes her as well! And why not? She is so pretty…now's my chance!' So Kamadeva drew out his bow and an arrow of garlands, took an aim…and struck! The arrow had **hit its mark**!

On the other hand, in the grove, Lord Shiva himself had been **struck** by Parvati's **incredible** beauty. With great difficulty, however, he went back to meditating. Just as he was about to close his eyes, he felt something soft had hit him. He looked down and saw the arrow of flowers.

Lord Shiva **fumed**, 'Who dares disturb me while I meditate!' He screamed and spotted Kamadeva hiding behind a tree, 'HOW

DARE YOU **COMMIT** SUCH A SHAMEFUL ACT?' And before Kamadeva could say anything, Lord Shiva opened his third eye and turned the God of Love to ashes!

Rati, seeing the **wrathful** or *raudra* avatar of Lord Shiva, fainted on the spot. Lord Shiva was so **indignant** at Kamadeva's action that he **stalked off** without even looking at Parvati.

Parvati felt deeply hurt and ashamed. Crying, she went back to her parents' house, with the **resolve** to forget about the incident and her love. But that was easier said than done! Parvati could not **divert** her attention from Lord Shiva. Finally, she went to her mother and said, 'Mother, I cannot live without Lord Shiva. I know he is upset due to the death of his wife. But I am not going to give up. I am going to the jungle to begin a severe penance. Maybe then he will realise that my **devotion** to him is complete and he will change his mind.' Himavat and Menaka were both against the idea. But they saw their daughter's firm resolve and agreed.

Meanwhile when Rati regained consciousness and realised her husband was no more, she wanted to kill herself. But just then, she heard a **celestial** voice **proclaim**, 'Live, O Rati. Do not kill yourself. Your husband will be brought back to life when Parvati and Lord Shiva get married. Do not worry!'

Rati found some comfort when she heard this but she still wondered, 'That poor child. How will she ever make such a grim and **terrifying** god fall in love with her?'

4
Parvati's Penance

So strong was Parvati's decision to win Lord Shiva's love that no one could stop her. She gave up her life of comfort. She removed all her lovely **ornaments**. She changed her **attire** too. Instead of soft and silky garments, she covered herself with a simple, thin white cloth. After **bidding** her parents a **sorrowful** goodbye, Parvati **set off** to the jungle.

But she did not go alone. Her parents sent a maid to look after her. In the jungle, Parvati had **made up her mind** to live like a hermit, doing all her work by herself. She slept on the cold, damp ground in her only white cloth. She did not even cover herself with a blanket!

She would eat **meagerly** and went hungry most of the time. Parvati spent her whole day in **solitude**, with only the animals for **company**. But mostly, she would sit under a tree quietly, **chanting** Lord Shiva's name. She was so **engrossed** in her prayers that even the other hermits would come and watch her.

Gradually, Parvati's penance became tougher and tougher. As days went by, she stopped eating completely. She thought that

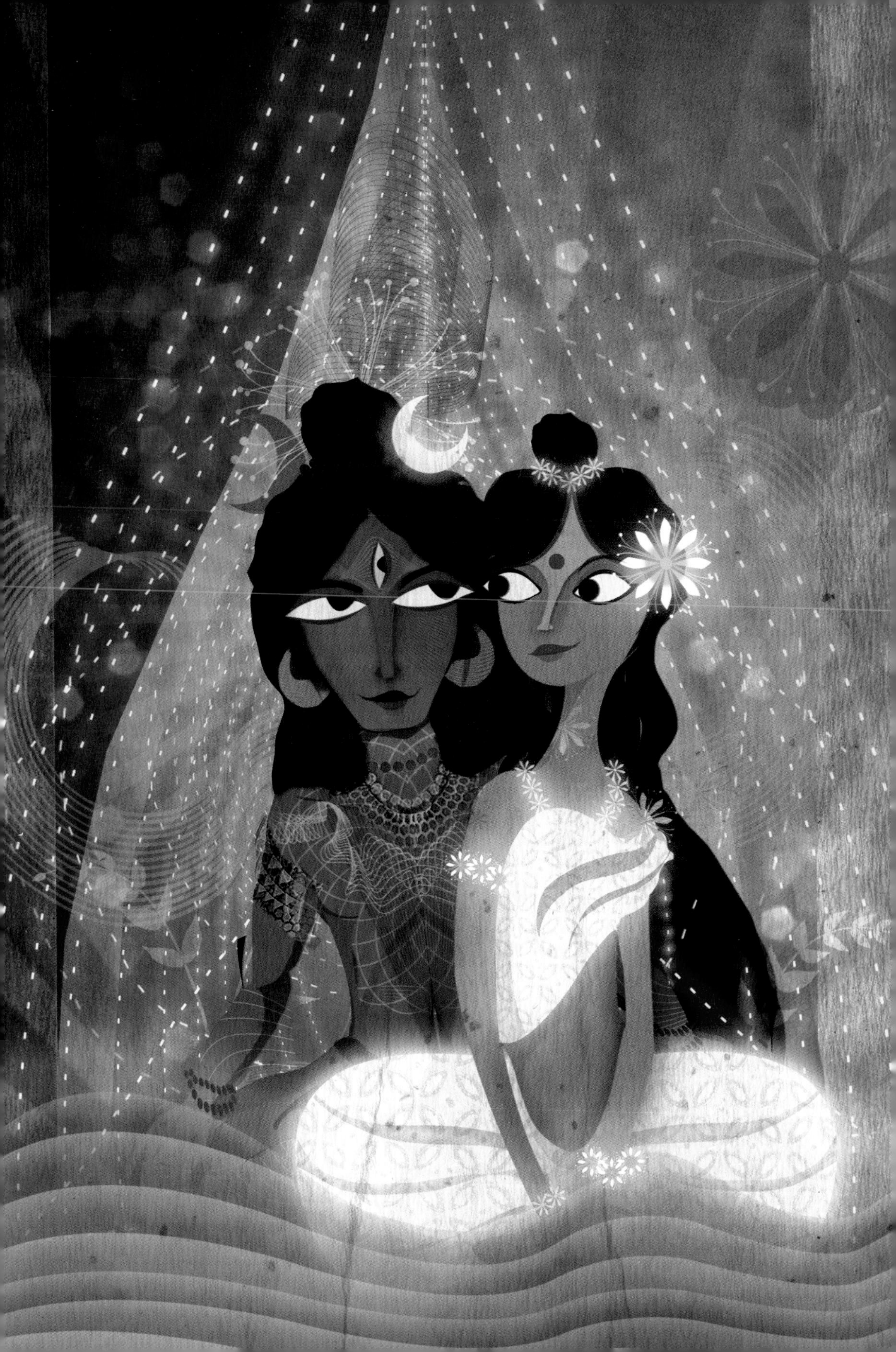

repeating the Lord's name would be enough to satisfy her hunger. The other hermits saw this and whispered among themselves, 'This gentle lady is truly devoted. Why, she has given up food! From this day on, she should be **addressed** as Aparna (the lady of the unbroken **fast**).'

As time **wore on**, Parvati changed her position. From sitting under a tree, she now began meditating while she sat in an icy pool of water! But through all her tough **rituals**, Lord Shiva did not once make an appearance. Parvati, though, was not **disheartened**.

Her many years of harsh life had only made her more beautiful.

After a very long time, one day, a sage or a *rishi* approached Parvati. He said, 'Dear lady. I have been observing you for a long time now. How and why has someone like you started so hard a penance? It is common enough for the lonely, the **grief-stricken** or the old to give up their life for this kind of *sannyas*. But you? Why? Surely you have not lived long enough to **experience** much sorrow?'

Parvati listened **patiently** while this kind and gentle sage **expressed** his worry for her. He went on, 'I **implore** you. Please stop. I feel **distressed** when I see you living like this. If you stop now, I will give you half of my **merits** which I have achieved through meditation!' Now Parvati was very confused. Her maid, who was seated nearby, then **acquainted** the sage about Parvati's decision.

The sage was **incredulous** when he heard this, 'Lord Shiva? Why, I have seen him with my own eyes. How can someone like you **yearn** for his love? He is so unclean and **foul-smelling**! Even his clothes are dirty. He is always covered in ashes and wears a

19

serpent around his neck. What could you possibly see in so **crude** a person? He is not meant for you. You deserve someone better.'

Every **insult** uttered against Lord Shiva hurt Parvati, though she continued to listen to the sage. Finally, she could not take it anymore and turning to the sage screamed, 'Do you dare to utter such **vile** words about so great a god? Stop now, O sage. Do not say another word. It takes a pure soul to recognise another. **Appearances** mean nothing to me.' She ordered her maid to ask him to leave the place immediately. Her **rage** was becoming **uncontrollable** and she could not **stand** his presence any longer.

Parvati was about to walk away from the spot when the sage blocked her path. She looked at him in anger and before her very eyes, something **astonishing** happened. The sage had turned into Lord Shiva himself!

Lord Shiva saw her surprise and smiled, 'Dear Parvati, your penance and devotion have won me over. I bow to your greatness. Please do me the honour and be my wife.'

Parvati's happiness knew no bounds. She turned to him and said, 'I'd be honoured. But you will have to ask my father for my hand in marriage.'

Lord Shiva agreed and soon sent seven of the most learned sages (*saptarishis*) to Lord Himavat's house with a marriage **proposal**. Lord Himavat was delighted and gave his blessings. Lord Shiva and Parvati's wedding was **solemnised** amidst great **pomp and show**. All the gods rejoiced at such a beautiful **union**. They were **ecstatic** to see Lord Shiva come out of his **intense** grief. Lord Shiva himself, content and happy, brought Kamadeva back to life.

So it was that Lord Shiva found his **soulmate** in Parvati and

they went to live on Mount Kailasa.

5
The Birth of Kartikeya

Goddess Parvati and Lord Shiva were happily living together on Mount Kailasa. The gods were also **relieved** that Lord Shiva could now help them in their war against Tarakasura.

They now knew it was only a matter of time before the divine couple had their first child and were eagerly waiting to hear some good **tidings**. But several years passed by and still Lord Shiva and Goddess Parvati were childless. Tarakasura on the other hand continued to trouble the gods, even after he had won the war. Lord Indra and others began to wonder whether Lord Brahma's **prediction** would ever come true.

Worried and anxious, the gods went to Lord Vishnu for help. Lord Indra said, 'O Lord, we do not know how to **deal** with cruel Tarakasura. We feel **hapless** against him. It has been many years now and we have not heard any news of a son being born to Lord Shiva and Goddess Parvati. This child was supposed to lead us in the war. Lord Shiva was our only hope.'

Lord Vishnu **soothed** Lord Indra, 'Be patient, O Indra. Everything will happen only when it is supposed to. Just remember,

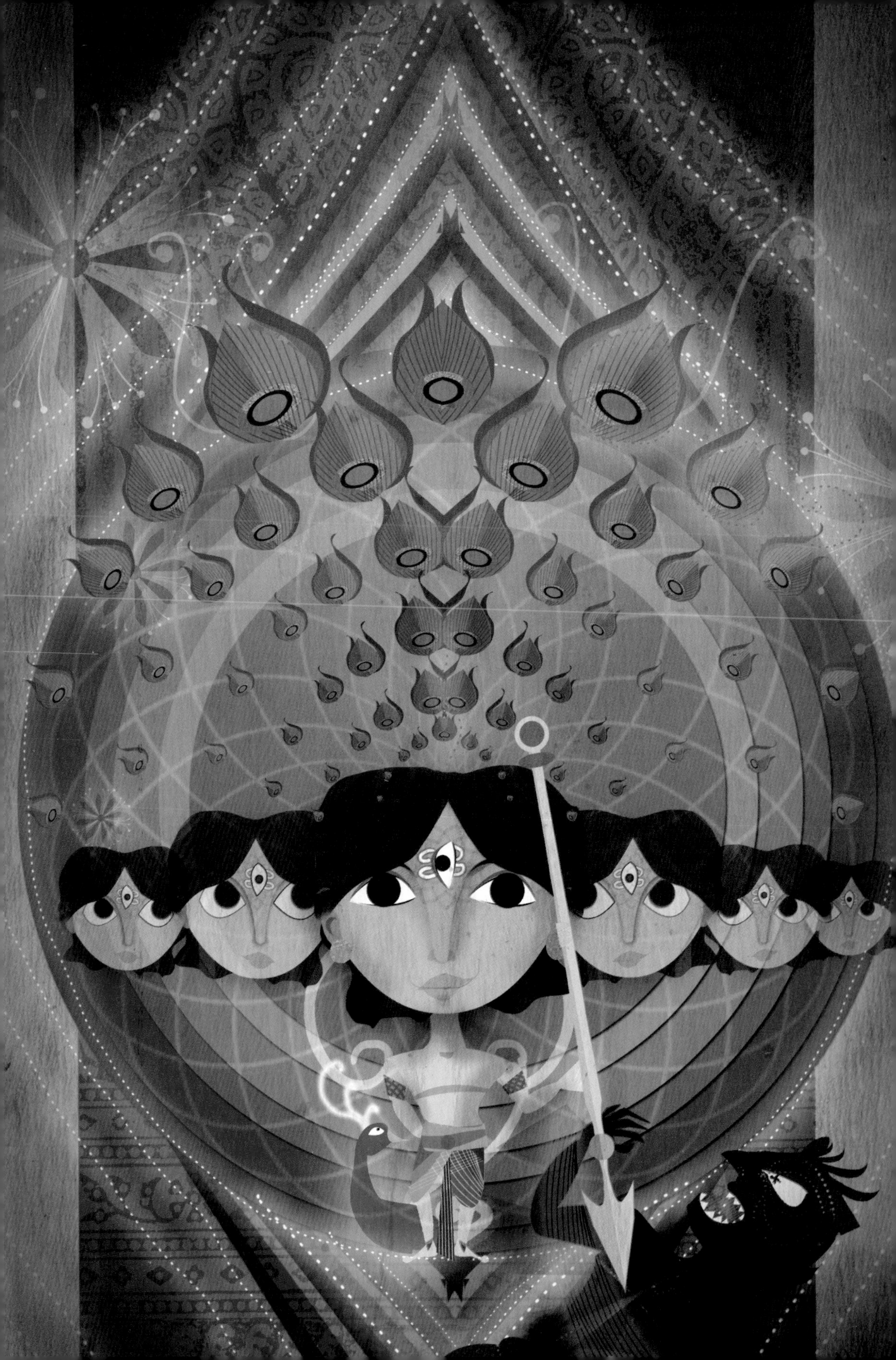

when the time is right, all of you should be ready to **hold on to** the seed of life that Lord Shiva will give you.' The gods went away **assured**. But soon their patience **ran out**, despite Lord Vishnu's words. They decided to pay a visit to Lord Shiva and Goddess Parvati at their abode on Mount Kailasa. Lord Shiva saw the gods approach and greeted them warmly, 'What brings you here today?'

'O Lord Shiva,' Lord Indra said **restlessly**, 'We require your help urgently. We cannot **tolerate** Tarakasura anymore. He has become uncontrollable. You are aware, I am sure, that Lord Brahma had once predicted that only your son would be able to destroy Tarakasura? We really need your help!'

'Yes, of course, I know about this prediction,' said Lord Shiva. 'Do not worry. I will rescue you from the **clutches** of the demon's rule.' So saying, Lord Shiva held out his hand and announced, 'I have here the seed of life. Whoever is capable of holding it should grab it.'

Just as he was about to release it, Agnideva took the form of a bird and swallowed the seed. Lord Shiva then blessed him and **declared**, 'One day the seed will become ripe. It will grow into a young boy—my child and your saviour.'

All this time, Goddess Parvati was watching the proceedings very carefully. When Agnideva grabbed hold of the seed, she screamed, 'You use such **unnatural** means to produce my son! Your impatience and hurry has caused you to disobey the laws of Nature!' The gods felt terribly **guilty** when they heard her but they were also relieved to finally have the answer to their problems. They left Mount Kailasa and went to Heaven.

Soon it was dinner time, and they sat down to eat a nice quiet meal. Agnideva supplied his fire to cook the food and the gods ate to their heart's content. But alas, their problems were far from over! Something strange began to happen after they had eaten their meal and were resting. They started complaining of severe stomach ache!

When Agnideva had given fire to prepare the food, the parts of the seed he had swallowed had **transferred** from his fire to the food, which the gods had eaten! While they were crying out in pain, they suddenly remembered Parvati's words. They then realised this had happened because the Goddess, in all **likelihood**, had cursed them!

They went back to the divine couple seeking forgiveness. They begged Goddess Parvati for mercy and appealed her to release them from this **torture**. She took pity on them and agreed to help. So Lord Shiva ordered the gods to spit out the food. They followed his instructions and soon began to feel better. All but Agnideva, who continued to feel the **gnawing** pain! Lord Shiva soothed him, 'Tomorrow early morning, hand over my seed to a woman. You will find her near the **banks** of the Ganga, taking a **predawn** bath.'

The next day, without wasting any time, Agnideva went to the river bank. There he discovered not one, but six women taking a dip in the holy Ganga! These women were Kritikas and wives of six sages. Agnideva then had an idea. He took the form of a **bonfire** and the women gathered around him to get some warmth. Soon, the sparks of the fire passed on the seed, in small parts, to the stomachs of all the six women!

Agnideva finally felt better but the poor women! Their stomachs **swelled** as though they were pregnant. They went to the foothills of the Himalayas where they rested. They were feeling sick, and **threw up** all the food they had eaten. Little did they know that the parts of the seed that had entered their bodies from the bonfire also came out now!

The seed **emanated** so much energy that even the mountain was unable to hold it! It threw the seed into the waters of the Ganga! Ganga's water immediately began to boil and the river threw the seed on its banks. The seed finally found **shelter amid** some **reeds** and that was where it lay in peace.

One day, when Lord Shiva and Goddess Parvati were walking along the banks of the Ganga, they passed by a shelter and saw a healthy baby **gurgling** away! The baby had six heads and Goddess Parvati recognised the infant as her very own son, born from Lord Shiva's seed.

She **tenderly** held him in her arms and gave him the name Kartikeya.

Even at birth, Karitkeya was no ordinary baby! He had twelve hands and there was a heavenly light surrounding his little body. He already held three weapons in his tiny hands and had the looks of a **warrior** even for a baby. The couple took their little son to the Kailasa where all gods came bearing gifts. Then Lord Shiva with Parvati sitting next to him said to Lord Indra, 'My dear Indra. Your wait is over. Kartikeya will lead you to victory against Tarakasura.'

Tarakasura too heard these words and began assembling an army, though he was sure that a mere baby would not be able to harm him, the demon king! But was he proved wrong!

When he was just seven days old, Kartikeya led the gods in a battle against Tarakasura and killed him. Heaven was free from the demon's cruelty all because of Kartikeya, Lord Shiva and Goddess Parvati's firstborn!

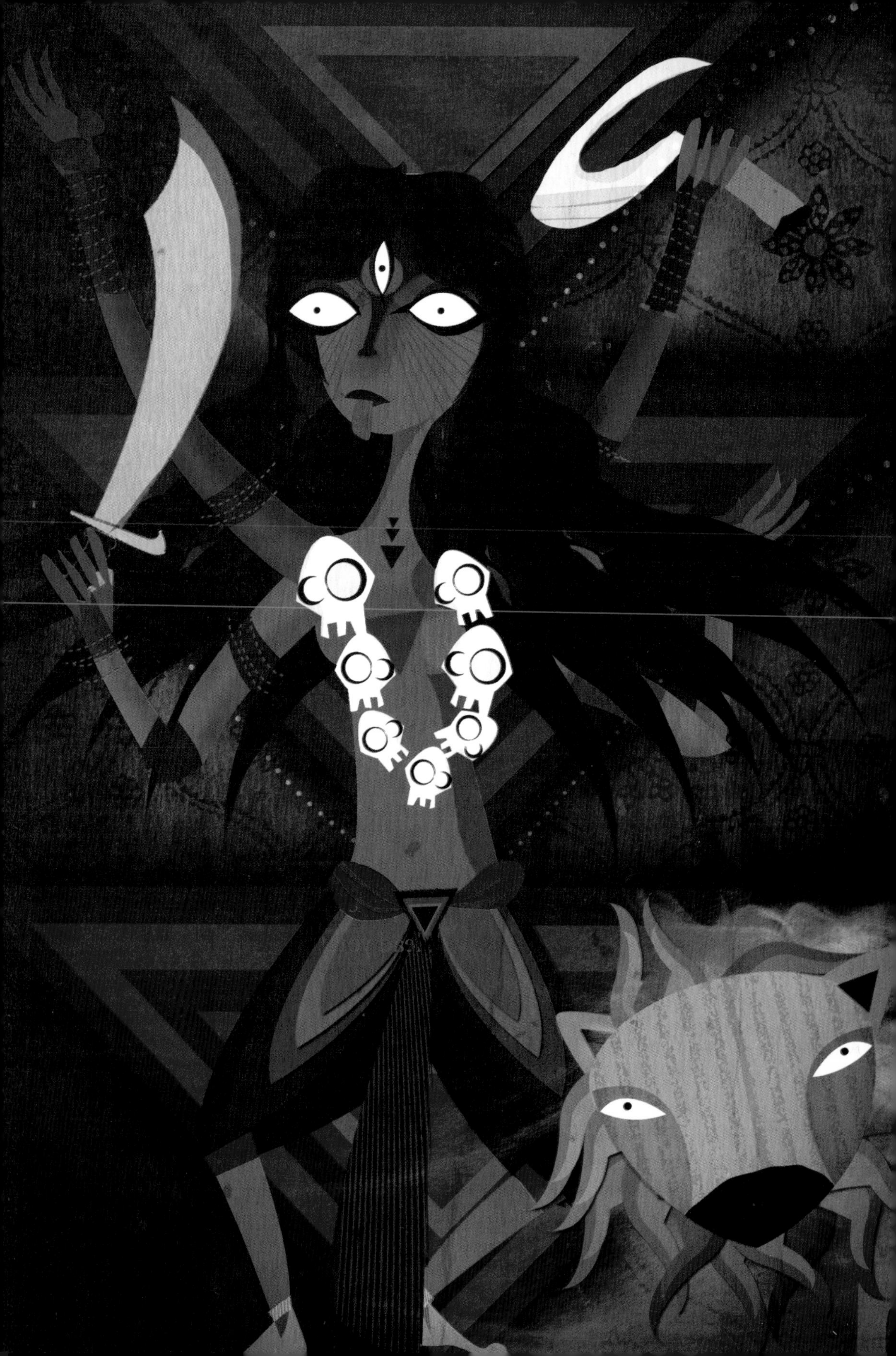

6
The Creation of Kali

Long ago, two extremely powerful demon brothers, Shumbha and Nishumbha, wanted to rule over the three worlds—Heaven, Earth and Netherworld. To fulfill their desire, they decided to pray to Lord Brahma. After they had successfully completed their penance, Lord Brahma had no choice but to appear before them. He granted them the boon that no man or god would be able to kill them. They would die only at the hands of a woman. **Satisfied**, Shumbha and Nishumbha then went off happily to plan their attack and fulfill their **goal**.

Lord Brahma was now truly **in a fix**. He knew what the two brothers were capable of. He thought, 'Only Lord Shiva can help me. I must meet him immediately.' Lord Brahma briefed Lord Shiva about the events. 'We must do everything to stop them. There is only one person who can help us, Goddess Parvati. You have to somehow make her so angry that in her rage, she creates a **supreme** power or shakti. This supreme power will be the protector of the gods for **eternity**.'

27

Lord Shiva gave his **consent**. He went back to his abode and thought of an idea. While they were both resting, Lord Shiva began teasing his wife about her skin colour. At first, Goddess Parvati ignored him but he simply would not stop! She then became extremely angry, 'My Lord, if you do not like my skin, I have no use for it. I will **shed** my skin with the blessings of Lord Brahma.' Lord Shiva was **taken aback**! His plan had **backfired**!

He tried to **convince** her that he had just been teasing her, but she would not listen. So she took his leave and Lord Shiva **sighed**, 'My dear wife, if this is what you wish to do, you have my blessings.'

Goddess Parvati went off to a **secluded** grove and began meditating to please Lord Brahma. Suddenly, there appeared before her a **fierce** tiger. **Growling** wildly, he looked ready to attack her. Goddess Parvati though, was not afraid at all. She thought that the tiger had come there to protect her from other wild animals. She went back to meditating. After staring at her for some time, the tiger itself lost its **appetite**! It became her **devotee** and stood guard by her side to protect her from other animals.

Meanwhile Lord Brahma decided that he himself must do something. He had not expected Goddess Parvati to behave like this! So he appeared before her. 'Dear Parvati. You have to stop this now. You have more important **deeds** awaiting you. The evil demon brothers Shumbha and Nishumbha have to die by your hands. The world needs to be saved from their **tyranny**. **Cease** now and go back to Mount Kailasa!'

Hearing these words, Goddess Parvati immediately got up. She closed her eyes and shook herself and **lo and behold**! She had shed her outer skin, which lay **crumpled** at her feet! Goddess

Parvati's skin had now acquired a golden colour. Due to this change she came to be known as Gauri, the Goddess with a golden skin. She bowed to Lord Brahma who gave her his blessings.

The dark skin that the Goddess had **cast off** then came together and a beautiful but terrifying form came to life. This was Goddess Kali, the dark and beautiful supreme power, the protector of the gods. Lord Brahma blessed Goddess Kali and provided her with several weapons. He also gave her a lion as her mount.

Whenever evil would **rear its head**, Goddess Parvati would take on the form of Goddess Kali and protect the good and the **virtuous**.

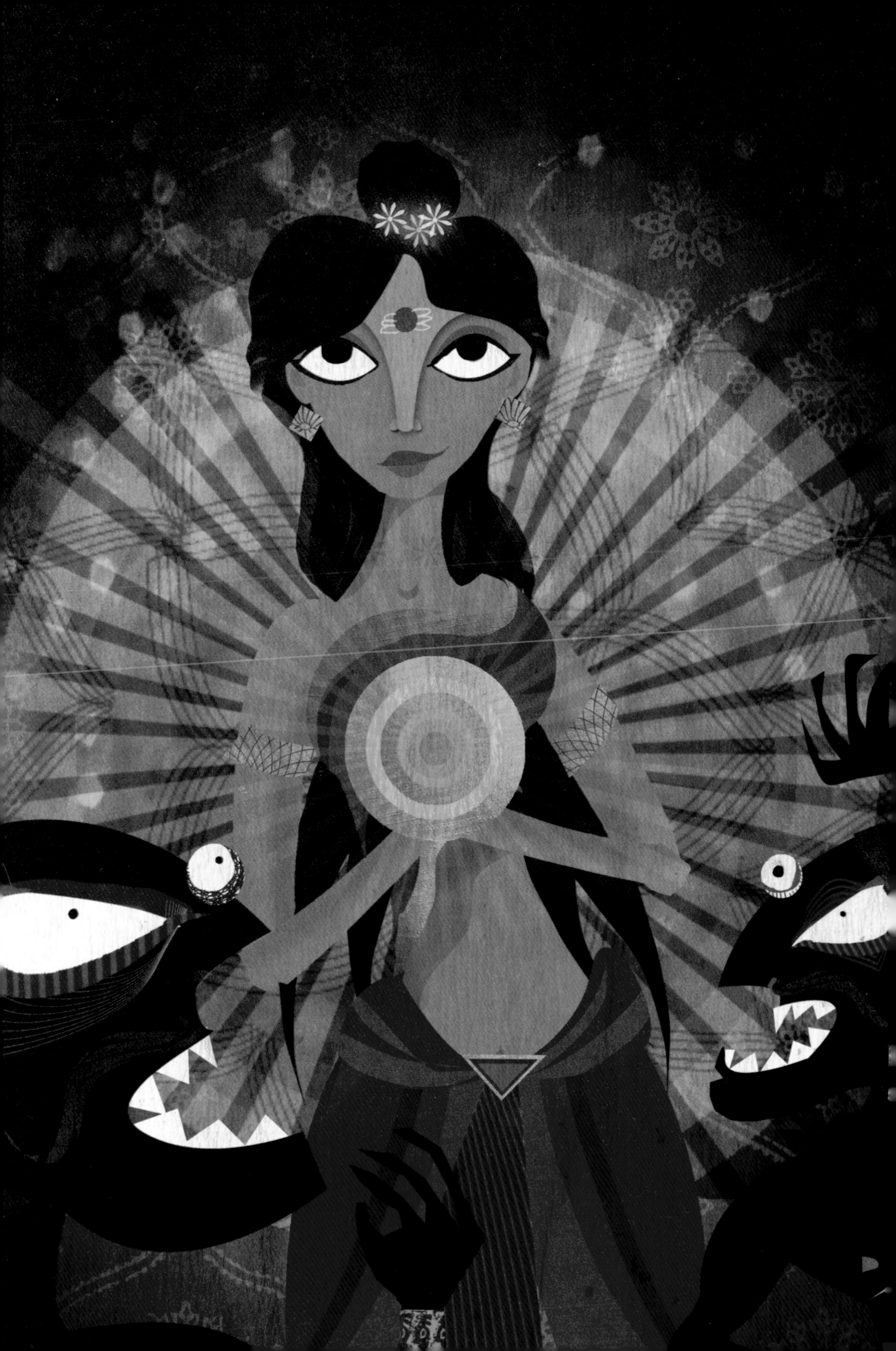

7

Demons Vidala and Utpala

Long ago, several demons **aspired** to defeat the gods and rule over Heaven and mankind. Vidala and Utpala were such powerful evil demons. The brothers were very cruel and wanted to spread their **empire** all through the universe.

In order to achieve this, they thought it best to first become immortal. They began to offer prayers to Lord Brahma for his blessings. When Lord Brahma appeared before them, he told them that apart from Lord Shiva, no one could **attain** immortality. So Vidala and Utpala had to be happy with the boon that no one but a woman could kill them. After all, who had ever heard of a woman fighting battles? In their arrogance, they firmly believed that nothing and nobody could now stop them.

Armed with pride and a will to **usurp** the power of gods, Vidala and Utpala launched a massive attack on Heaven. The gods lost the battle and the **victorious duo** returned to their kingdom. They were busy in celebrating their **conquest** when Narad Muni, the divine sage, **paid them a visit**. He offered his greetings and said, 'My dear lords. You have proved to the entire universe that you are the most powerful and **accomplished** rulers in existence.' Vidala and Utpala were both delighted to hear such words of praise. Narad Muni then went on to tell them about all the gods, particularly about the holy trinity of Lord Brahma, Lord Vishnu and Lord Shiva. While describing Lord Shiva and his wife's love for each other, Narad Muni **sang praises** of Goddess Parvati's beauty. Both the demons were curious to know more about her.

After Narad Muni left, Vidala told his brother, 'This Parvati, if she is as beautiful as Narad Muni describes her, she should be part of our kingdom. After all, we are the rulers of the three worlds. What is she doing with someone like Lord Shiva?'

'You are right,' Utpala replied. 'Once we show her our immense wealth and great **prowess**, she will be impressed. But first, we should go and see whether she really is as **graceful** and charming. We will kidnap her as soon as we see her. This way, she won't have a chance to protest!'

And so Vidala and Utpala set off looking for her. They decided to take the air route first as there was no hazard of being caught **sneaking**. Lord Shiva and Goddess Parvati already knew what was going on. Narad Muni had warned them in advance. They were ready to deal with the two demons. While they were flying over Kashi, they saw a beautiful maiden playing with a ball along with her friends. When they saw her laughing and enjoying, they were struck by her **comeliness**. They concluded that this was indeed the **beauteous** Goddess Parvati herself. They resolved to take her away!

They came flying down and with their powers, **disguised** themselves as two of Lord Shiva's soldiers. They began walking towards Goddess Parvati. Lord Shiva was hiding in the **vicinity** to keep a watch on the **cunning** devils. He saw the two demons approaching his wife and signalled her to be ready.

Goddess Parvati saw the two demons. She had the ball in her hands and with a mighty force, threw it hard in the direction of Vidala and Utpala. The two of them were surprised and extended their hands to catch the ball. The moment their hands made a contact with it, however, they fell on the ground, dead!

The two **wicked** demons had indeed died at the hands of a woman, just as Lord Brahma's boon had proclaimed!

The ball after killing the two demons, turned into a *shivalinga*, which remains at the spot in the Himalayas to this day. This *shivalinga* is known as Kandukeshwara.

8
Ganesha Gets an Elephant Head

Lord Shiva and Goddess Parvati were **well settled** in their abode on Mount Kailasa. Their guards and maids were **devoted** to them. But while Lord Shiva had his **trusted** guard and **confidant** Nandi, Goddess Parvati herself did not have anyone.

One day, it so happened that Goddess Parvati was busy having a bath when Lord Shiva suddenly entered her room without any **prior** warning. She was very **annoyed** at being disturbed, even by her own husband! 'I need a guard of my own too. Someone who will warn me when people are coming and be with me at all times,' she thought to herself.

She was staring off into space wondering what to do when she had an idea. While she was taking bath, she created the statue out of the **cosmetic** paste that she was using. This statue was exactly like a living person. He had a beautiful, child-like face. But he was not just a child. When Goddess Parvati brought him to life, the statue became a warrior. He already knew how to use weapons while fighting the enemy!

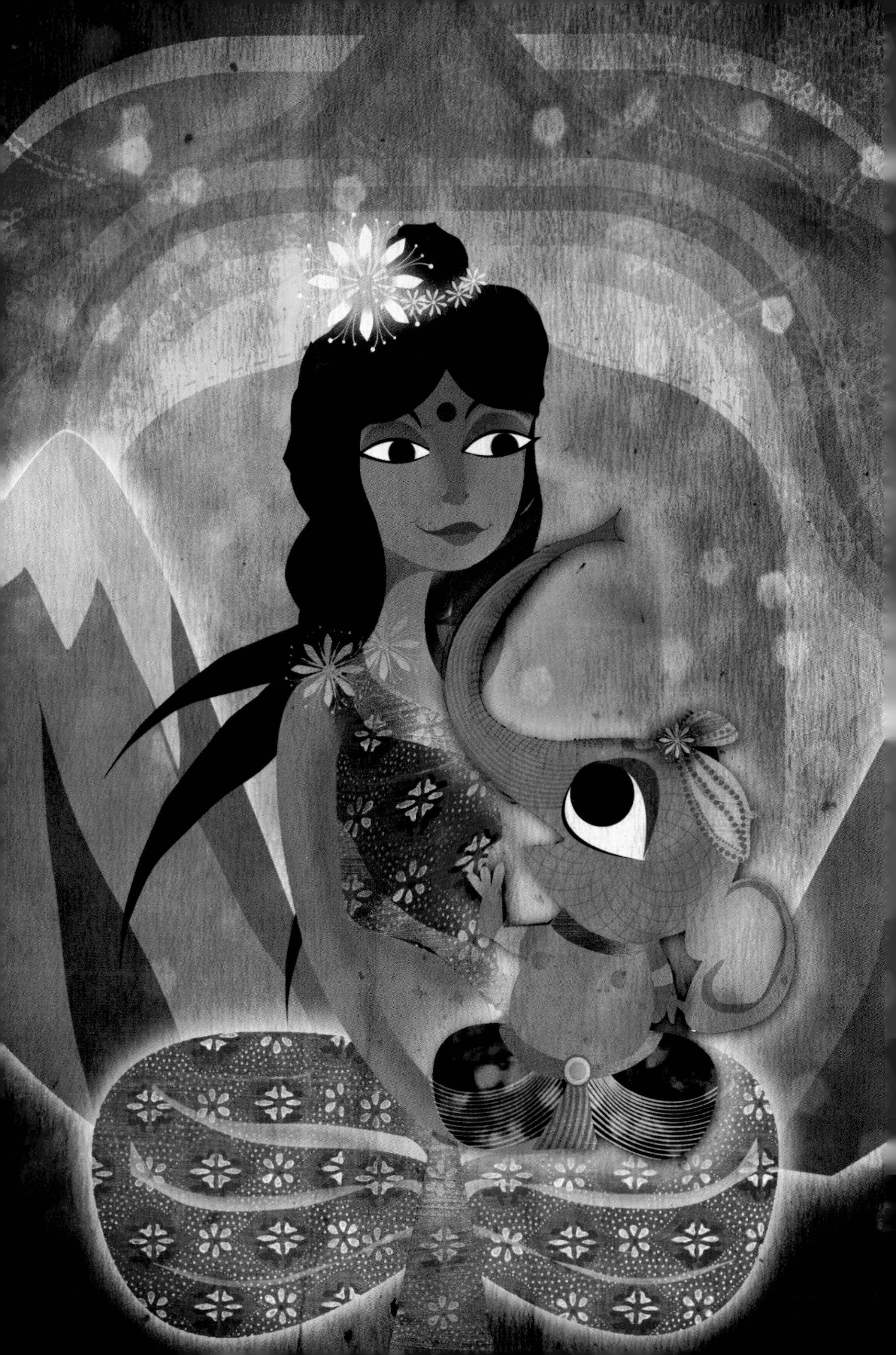

The Goddess was delighted at her creation and ordered the little boy warrior to stand guard outside her room. He was not to let anyone enter without first checking with her. She named this boy Ganesha and began to **shower** love and affection on him as though he was her son. One day, Lord Shiva again dropped by his wife's rooms without informing her. Goddess Parvati was busy in some other important activities and had instructed Ganesha to not let anyone disturb her.

When Lord Shiva reached his beloved wife's room and saw a small child standing guard outside, he did not think much of it. As he tried to enter, Ganesha stopped him, 'Wait, dear sir. You cannot enter.'

Lord Shiva was **irritated**. He looked at Ganesha and **thundered**, 'Who are you to stop me. I am Lord Shiva. This is my house and the lady within is my wife. I shall do as I please!' But Ganesha was very **stubborn**. He had, after all, been given a duty to not let anyone enter. He was going to obey the orders given to him.

Lord Shiva was again stopped from entering. Angry, he walked off from there, thinking to himself, 'I am going to teach that boy a lesson!' He then sent two of his strong guards to fight with Ganesha, but imagine his surprise when the little child defeated his experienced guards!

Lord Shiva didn't give up and sent a stronger **force** this time. But even they came back **vanquished**. Now Lord Shiva was truly **livid**. How could a small boy keep him out of his own house! And how could his affectionate Parvati allow this to happen!

Finally, Lord Shiva himself decided to sort it out with the boy. And what a battle it was! Lord Shiva was not finding it easy to defeat Ganesha and the fight went on for very long.

Ultimately, Lord Shiva's **superior** ability was too much for Ganesha to handle. Lord Shiva in his intense anger chopped off little Ganesha's head.

When Goddess Parvati emerged from her room and saw her dear son lying dead, her anger was uncontrollable. Even Lord Shiva started feeling very guilty and sorrowful for what he had done. The Goddess was so angry that she took on her wrathful form and was ready to destroy the entire universe—even the gods! From her anger emerged a number of goddesses who started swallowing things around them! The gods were all **cowering** with fear.

Lord Shiva, Narad Muni and other gods approached the indignant Goddess and **tendered** their apologies to her. They had to calm her down otherwise the world would have come to an end! 'Please O great Devi. Forgive us! We have committed a sin. Give us a chance to fix this!' Thankfully her temper calmed down and she declared, 'The only way to fix this is to bring my son Ganesha back to life. And when he is alive again, he should be worshipped before Lord Brahma, Lord Vishnu and Lord Shiva himself.'

All the gods readily agreed. Ganesha was after all, a great warrior and one who had kept his word even in the face of so much **opposition**. Lord Shiva then ordered his guards and other gods, 'Go. Go now and bring me the first head that you find! Do not delay!'

Now the gods were in a fix. How were they going to find a head? They decided to seek Lord Vishnu's assistance. After all, he was the **omniscient** one and their protector. Lord Vishnu agreed to help them out in this task. He set off in search of a head. He kept on wandering for long and finally came upon a dead elephant whose head had been cut off. He gave it to the gods who took the head back to Mount Kailasa and attached it to Ganesha's body. Goddess Parvati was very happy to see her son brought back to life. Lord Shiva himself was glad to see Ganesha alive and his Parvati back to her gentle self.

So it was that Lord Shiva and Goddess Parvati's younger son, Ganesha, got the head of an elephant!

9
Parvati Tests Lord Rama

Once Lord Shiva and Goddess Parvati decided to leave their home on Mount Kailasa and find out what was happening on Earth. Their journey took them along river banks, over mountain tops, through valleys and plains and **dense** jungles. Once, while they were walking through a thick jungle, the Goddess saw two strangers walking hurriedly in their direction. They were both dressed in simple **robes** with no **finery**. Goddess Parvati thought they were hermits who were living in the jungle.

But when they came closer, she realised they each carried a bow and had a **quiver** full of arrows **strapped** to their backs. Both the men appeared to be very nervous and tense. However, they stopped when they saw Lord Shiva and Goddess Parvati, and bowed respectfully before hurrying off. What surprised the Goddess was that Lord Shiva had also **responded** to the strangers' greetings in the same **reverential** manner!

Now Goddess Parvati was truly confused. She turned to Lord Shiva and asked, 'Dear Lord, why did you bow to two simple hermits?' Lord Shiva laughed and replied, 'My dear wife, they

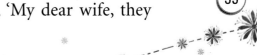

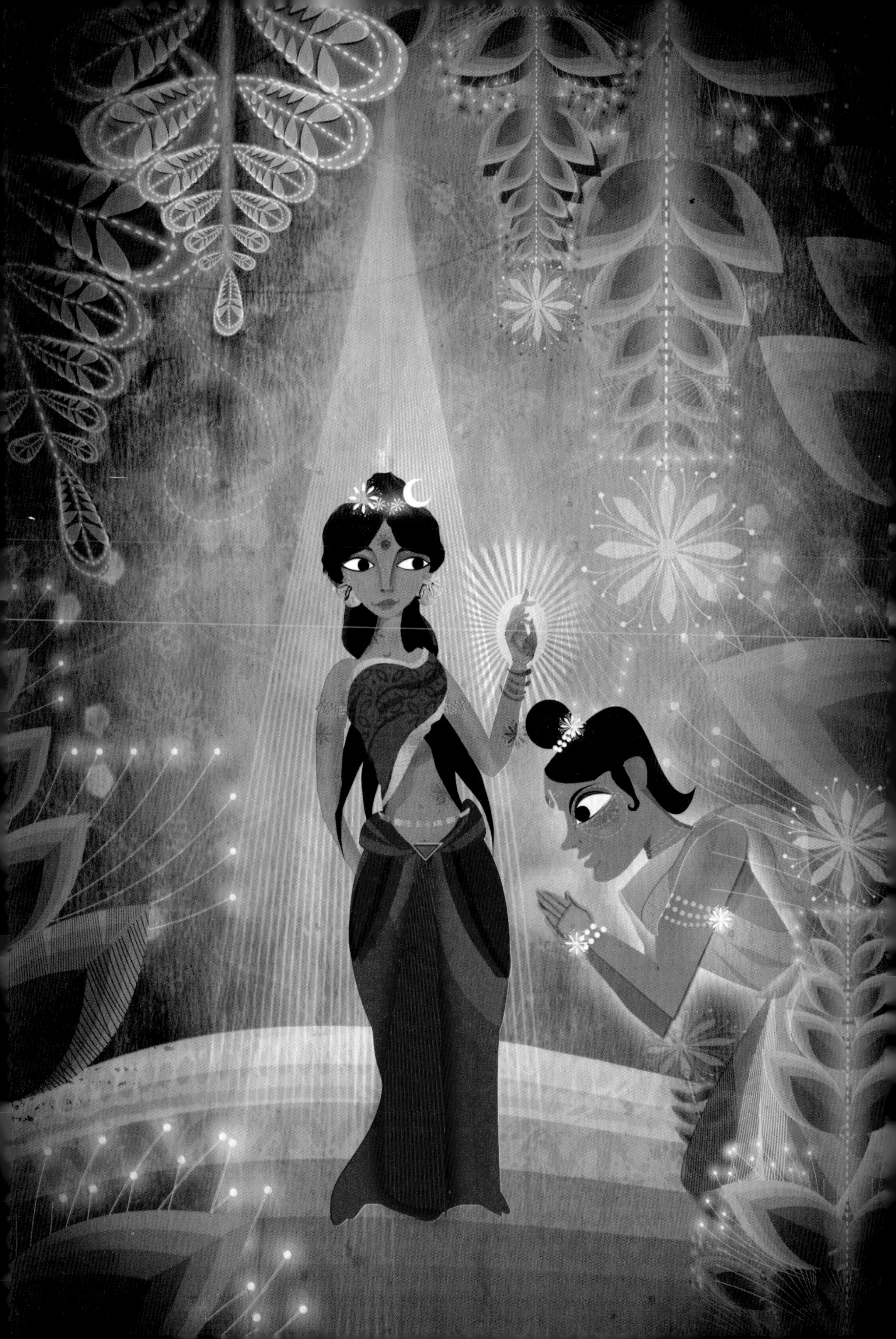

are not simple hermits! That was Lord Rama and his brother Lakshmana. And Rama is none other than Lord Vishnu who has taken birth on Earth!'

Lord Shiva then acquainted her about Sita and Lord Rama and Sita's **abduction** by Ravana, the demon king of Lanka. 'Lord Rama is now searching for her. He is completely devoted to his wife.' Parvati expressed her doubts about this. 'But if he is Lord Vishnu as you say, finding Sita should be easy for him! Why go through so much trouble? Are you certain about this?'

Pat came the reply from Lord Shiva, 'Why don't you test him and find out for yourself?' Instantly, Goddess Parvati disguised herself as Sita and set off to find Lord Rama.

She had not gone far when she saw him. She quietly walked up to him. Goddess Parvati was confident that Lord Rama would not be able to see through her disguise. Rather he would be **overjoyed** to see his beloved wife. But Lord Rama greeted her with reverence, 'O Mother Parvati, why do you **grace** me with your presence alone? Why did Lord Shiva not come as well?'

Parvati was astonished! She was also rather **embarrassed**, 'Forgive me O Lord. I did not believe my husband's words about your real **identity**. I decided to check for myself.'

Lord Rama just smiled gently and said, 'O great Goddess, I am just a **mere mortal** doing my duty. There is nothing to apologise for! You honour me with your presence!' Goddess Parvati bowed and took her leave. Soon, she and Lord Shiva went back to Mount Kailasa. There Lord Shiva narrated the entire story of Lord Rama and his life in detail to Goddess Parvati.

Rapt in attention the Goddess heard the story, **secure** in the knowledge that Lord Vishnu indeed had taken birth as Lord Rama to vanquish the evil demon Ravana and save the world.

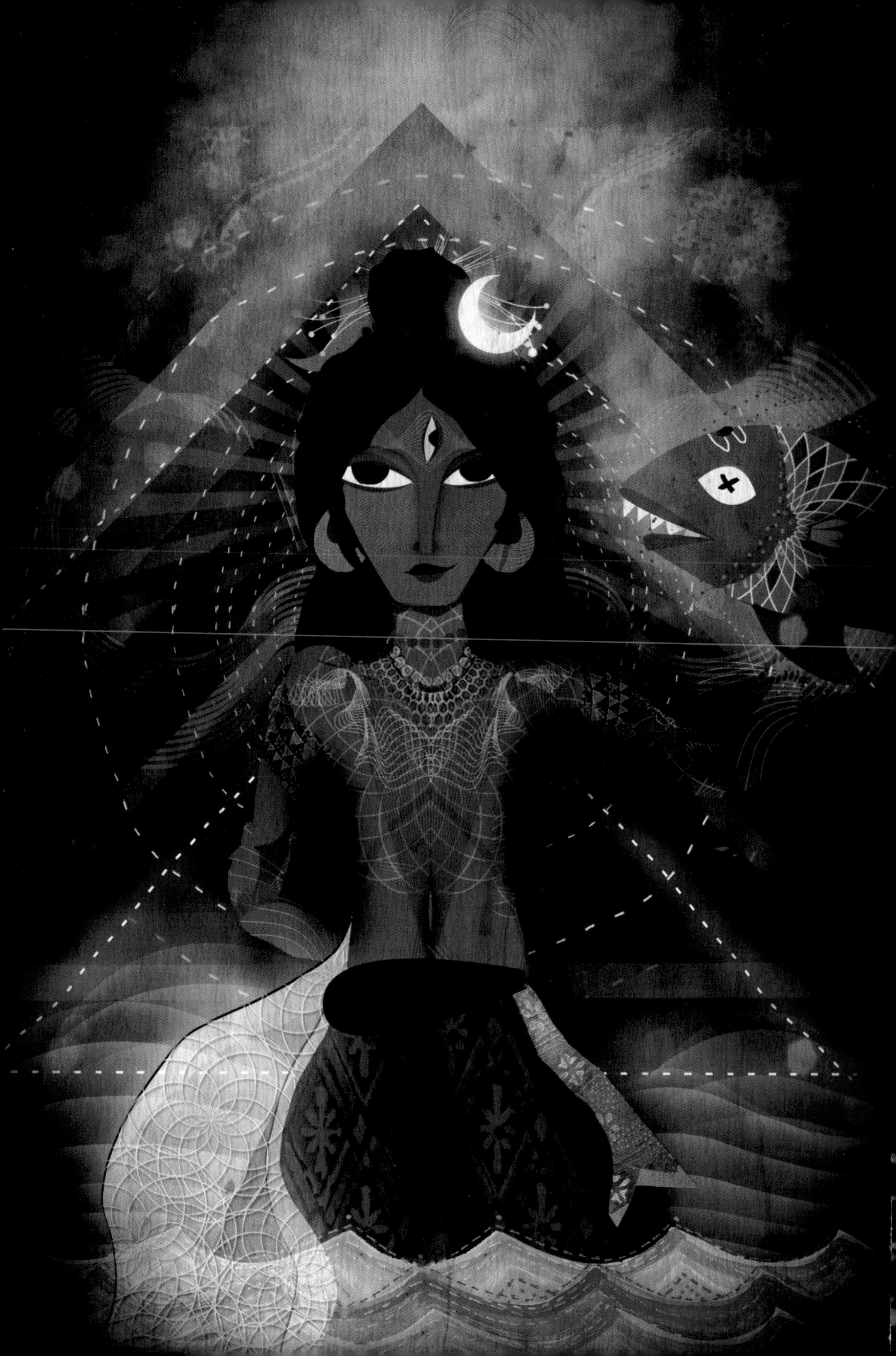

10
Fisherwoman Parvati
· ·

Lord Shiva once took it upon himself to explain the *Brahmandayana* (**mysteries** of the universe) to his wife. Goddess Parvati herself was very eager to learn all there was to know. And who better to teach her than the great Lord Shiva himself!

So Lord Shiva began to explain the story behind the **creation** of this vast universe to her. She listened very attentively at first, concentrating on what Lord Shiva was saying. The Goddess listened and listened and listened…and this went on for several years! But there was no end in sight to Lord Shiva's lesson. Finally, though she tried very hard, Goddess Parvati lost her focus. Lord Shiva saw this and was angry at his wife's sudden change in behaviour. 'Parvati, if what I say is boring you, I shall stop. If you cannot concentrate on something so important, you should have been born to fisherfolk so that you could do hard work and not think about such matters!'

The Goddess was hurt but Lord Shiva felt even worse for his harsh words. Alas, before he could do anything about it, Goddess Parvati had disappeared from their home! Lord Shiva felt extremely

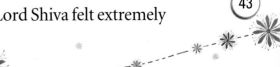

sad and **regretted** his words, 'How am I to live without my beloved wife?' he thought to himself.

His words had come true! Far away down on Earth, Goddess Parvati had taken birth as a baby girl and lay sheltered under a tree. Within no time, a **clan** of fisherfolk, the Parvaras, walked by and the chief saw this baby. He picked her up and was immediately **enchanted** by the baby's beauty, 'The gods have blessed me. What a lovely child! I will take her with me and bring her up as my own daughter.'

The chief brought the baby girl home. He named her Parvati. Little did he know that the baby he loved like his own child was in fact, the Goddess who was revered by all!

Soon Parvati grew to be a lovely girl. She would **accompany** her father on his boat as he went fishing. Everyone in the clan **adored** her. But the one who loved her most was far away on Mount Kailasa, **pining** for her and wondering how to get her back!

Lord Shiva was **disgruntled** at being alone in his abode. He could not bear the **separation** from the Goddess. Observing this, one day his trusted guard, Nandi, appealed to him, 'O dear Lord, why don't you go and bring her back? You know she is living with the Parvaras.'

But Lord Siva shook his head sorrowfully and replied, 'No Nandi. She was **reared** by fisherfolk and she will marry a fisherman in this life. That is the law of the world.' Sighing, he went back to his **brooding**.

Nandi, however, did not give up. He had a plan to unite his master and mistress.

He went down to Earth and taking the form of a shark, jumped into the sea. Then he set off for the coast where the Parvaras were living. Suddenly, two Parvaras fishermen out **at sea** saw this great big shark coming towards them. They started to turn away but it was too late. The shark had **capsized** the boat and the two fishermen fell into the water.

Over the next few days, the shark continued to trouble the fishermen. It tore their nets, **overturned** their boats and was a terrible **nuisance**. Finally, the chief called for a meeting and stated, 'Anyone who can capture this shark can **claim** my daughter's hand in marriage.'

Many brave young men tried but they all failed. Giving up hope, the Parvaras offered their prayers to the *shivalinga*. Parvati too prayed very hard, 'O Lord Shiva, please help us. We are all suffering because of this shark. Please help us.'

Lord Shiva, even in his sorrow, heard this voice and knew it was time to help the Parvaras. Besides, he would finally get to meet his wife! Taking the form of a young fisherboy, he went to the coastal village of the Parvaras and met the chief, 'I will stop this shark. Do not worry. It will not bother you after today.'

He then took a large net and **waded** into the water. Nandi, in his shark form, saw the young boy approach and recognised that he was none other than Lord Shiva. He smiled to himself, 'Ah! My Lord has come. My work here is now done.' He did not put up a fight when the boy threw the net over him.

Everyone in the clan rejoiced and was happy. Parvati too was glad that so **courageous** and skilled a fisherman was going to be her husband. The chief, as promised, gave Parvati's hand in marriage to the boy.

Lord Shiva had finally been united with his beloved wife and together they made their way back to Kailasa.

Glossary

p. 7   *Trinity*: a group of three
        Forego: give up
        Householder: a man who lives a family life
        Devastated: completely shattered
        Grove: a group of trees
        Hermit: a person who lives alone and meditates
        Absorbed: occupied
        Rejoicing: celebrating
        Consort: wife and companion

p. 8   *Avatar*: another form
        Penances: make apologies by doing something
        Knew no bounds: was beyond control
        Acquired: gained
        Ceremonial: royal
        Enraged: terrible anger
        Vowed: promised
        Pledge: oath
        Fulfillment: achievement

Charming: having qualities that attract people

Divine: heavenly

Instantly: right away

Recognised: was familiar with

Destined: something that is meant to happen in the future

Puzzled: confused

Ascetic: one who has completely given up comfort and luxury and lives all alone.

Appreciate: be grateful for

Concentrate: to pay close attention

Attend to: look after

p. 9 *Unaware*: not knowing

Unbeknownst: without someone being aware

Ripe: perfect or timely

Charge: command

Drove them out: threw them out

Crisis: an emergency

Counsel: advice

Harassing: troubling

Commander: chief

Fret: to be troubled

Risk: to take a chance in certain situations, knowing that the consequences may prove dangerous.

Shook off: got rid of

p. 11 *Woes*: problems

Euphoric: a state of great happiness

Edge over: to be in a better position than someone else

Conquered: defeated

Maiden: a young girl

Dared: did something bravely

Severe: harsh

Tremble: to shake because of fear

p. 12 *Shuddered*: shook with fear

Misdeed: wrong doing

Consulting: discussing

Appealing: pleading

Eventually: at long last; finally

Emerge: appear out of

Oblige: to be forced to do a favour

Immortal: someone who can never die

Grieving: feeling deep sorrow due to the death of a
loved one.

Worldly: to do with people and activities of the world

Mere infant: just a small baby

Mourning: acts or feelings that show great sorrow at
someone's death.

p. 13 *Plotting*: planning something secretly

Glance: a brief look

Gradually: slowly

Abode: residence

Narrated: told

Oblivious: not being aware of something

Saviour: someone who comes to the rescue of helpless
people.

p. 15 *Confided*: shared a secret

Unpredictable: something that is likely to change anytime

Radiant: glowing with joy

Reassured: gave support and comfort

Grim: to appear very serious

Hesitated: paused due to being unsure

Hit its mark: aim and hit the right place

Struck: impressed

Incredible: unbelievable

Fumed: to be in a state of great anger

p. 16 *Commit*: make

Wrathful: furious

Indignant: very angry

Stalked off: walked away in anger

Resolve: firm decision

Divert: to turn the focus away from a serious matter

Devotion: loyalty

Celestial: heavenly

Proclaim: announce

Terrifying: frightening

p. 17 *Ornaments*: jewellery

Attire: clothes

Bidding: saying

Sorrowful: sad

Set off: to begin a journey

Made up her mind: made a firm decision

Meagerly: very little

Solitude: being completely by oneself

Company: friends

Chanting: reading or saying something repeatedly in a
       sing-song manner.

Engrossed: to be busy with something

p. 19 *Addressed*: to use a particular name

Fast: to eat no food

Wore on: passed

Rituals: strict practices to follow

Disheartened: discouraged

Grief-stricken: broken-hearted

Sannyas: a state where a person lives like a hermit and gives up all relations with the world.

Experience: feel

Patiently: calmly

Expressed: made known

Implore: to request somebody to do something for you urgently.

Distressed: troubled

Merits: good points

Acquainted: told or informed

Incredulous: not able to believe something

Yearn: to long for something

Foul-smelling: bad-smelling

p. 20   *Serpent*: snake

Crude: someone with bad manners

Insult: to say something bad about someone

Vile: evil

Appearances: looks of a person

Rage: terrible anger

Uncontrollable: something that cannot be managed

Stand: bear

Astonishing: surprising

Proposal: offer

Solemnised: to perform a ceremony

Pomp and show: grand celebrations

Union: coming together

Ecstatic: delighted

Intense: deep

Soulmate: a person, husband or wife, who one loves very deeply and with whom one has a very strong attachment.

p. 21 *Relieved*: to be comforted

Tidings: news

Prediction: a statement made about the future

Deal: handle

Hapless: unfortunate

Soothed: comforted

p. 23 *Hold on to*: keep

Assured: confident

Ran out: finished

Restlessly: anxiously, nervously

Tolerate: put up with

Clutches: power

Declared: said something in a formal manner

Unnatural: not normal

Guilty: to be at fault

p. 24 *Transferred*: moved from one place to other

Likelihood: possibility, chance

Torture: terrible suffering and pain

Gnawing: continuous

Banks: along the shore of a river

Predawn: the time just before dawn

Bonfire: a large fire lit outdoors by collecting dry wood or tree branches.

Swelled: grew in size

Threw up: to vomit

p. 25 *Emanated*: gave out

Shelter: protection

Amid: in the middle

Reeds: tall grass with straight stalks that grows in wet areas.

Gurgling: a sound made by babies when they are happy

Tenderly: lovingly

Warrior: soldier

p. 27 *Satisfied*: Pleased

Goal: final aim

In a fix: to find oneself in a difficult situation

Supreme: highest

Eternity: a period of time that seems to last forever

p. 28 *Consent*: permission

Shed: get rid of

Taken aback: very surprised

Backfired: did not go as planned

Convince: to make someone agree on a matter

Sighed: let out a long breath due to sadness

Secluded: quiet and lonely

Fierce: frightening

Growling: a sound made by animals when they are about to attack.

Appetite: hunger

Devotee: follower

Deeds: actions

Tyranny: very cruel rule

Cease: stop at once

Lo and behold: suddenly before one's very eyes

Crumpled: crushed into folds

p. 29   *Cast off*: throw away

       Rear its head: become a problem that needs to be taken
            care of

       Virtuous: a person with good values

p. 31   *Aspired*: strongly desired

       Empire: Kingdom

       Attain: succeed to get something

       Usurp: grab with force

       Victorious: the one who wins

       Duo: a pair

       Conquest: to gain something after defeating the enemy

       Paid them a visit: an act of going to meet someone

p. 32   *Accomplished*: talented and skillful

       Sang praises: to speak well of somebody

       Prowess: great ability

       Graceful: beautiful

       Sneaking: moving in a secretive manner

       Comeliness: beauty

       Beauteous: beautiful

       Disguised: to dress up like somebody else in order to look
            different.

p. 33   *Vicinity*: area around a particular place

       Cunning: sly

       Wicked: evil

p. 34   *Well settled*: happily living one's life

       Devoted: loyal

       Trusted: loyal, reliable and responsible

       Confidant: a trusted and loyal friend with whom secrets
            are shared.

       Prior: before

Annoyed: angry

Cosmetic: a preparation for beautifying the face, skin, etc.

p. 36 *Shower*: to give in large amounts

Irritated: to be bothered, angry

Thundered: shouted loudly

Stubborn: not willing to change one's mind

Force: an army of soldiers

Vanquished: defeated

Livid: furious

p. 37 *Superior*: better than someone or something

Cowering: to crouch, bend down in fear

Tendered: offered

Opposition: a person or group who is against another person or group.

Omniscient: one who knows everything

p. 39 *Dense*: thick

Robes: long, loose garments

Finery: colourful clothes

Quiver: a container for arrows that is strapped across the back.

Strapped: tied

Responded: answered

Reverential: showing deep respect

p. 41 *Abduction*: act of kidnapping

Overjoyed: extremely happy

Grace: honour

Embarrassed: ashamed

Identity: name of a person

Mere mortal: just a human being

Rapt in attention: completely absorbed

Secure: without having a doubt

p. 43 *Mysteries*: things that are not known

Creation: refers to the entire universe

p. 44 *Regretted*: was sorry

Clan: a group of families who share customs, language, religion, etc.

Enchanted: to be charmed by something

Accompany: go along with someone

Adored: deeply loved and respected

Pining: missing someone

Disgruntled: angry, upset

Separation: a parting, not living together

Reared: to be brought up by parents or guardians

Brooding: thinking and worrying only about one subject

p. 45 *At sea*: in the middle of the sea

Capsized: turned upside down

Overturned: turned over

Nuisance: a person or thing that causes bother

Claim: take

Waded: walked into the water with effort

Courageous: brave